Papa Panov' Christmas

A play

Paul Thain

From a story by Leo Tolstoy

Samuel French - London
New York - Toronto - Hollywood

NOTES TO THE DIRECTOR

Let everything be as simple as possible. Atmosphere should be conveyed through light and sound, rather than elaborate stage furniture.

There's probably as much fun and learning opportunity in the preparation of the play as there is in its performance. And although the size of the cast need be limited only by the size of the acting area, some children will inevitably prefer to be involved in stage management.

All the children's skills and interests can be actively involved—simple, basic woodwork, designing and creation of costumes and make-up, and the disciplined execution of lighting plots and sound effects. There are also several opportunities for the creative use of musical instruments—the more strange and surreal the better.

Similarly, the dancing can be choreographed either in the Russian folk tradition or something devised by themselves. Ideally, the dance should include brief solo performances while the children (and the audience!) clap in rhythm.

Everyone should be able to find some place for their individual talents. The overall aim should be to combine the best elements of the traditional nativity play with those of traditional pantomime.

Paul Thain

For Miranda and Daniel

PAPA PANOV'S MAGIC CHRISTMAS

An acting area, partly raised if possible, representing Papa Panov's workshop. There is an "empty" door-frame, two chairs, a workbench and a cast-iron stove

In darkness, all the Children enter through the auditorium, each carrying a lighted candle, singing, "In Dulci Jubilo"

They sit themselves around the main acting area. Then, as their song ends, the Storyteller steps into the circle of golden candlelight

Storyteller Have you ever heard of Papa Panov?

The Children shake their heads

No? Well, he was certainly a very curious man. Most people thought he was mad, but there were a few—not many, it's true—but there were some who believed he had been blessed by God.

It all began one Christmas Eve many years ago, far, far away in a land called Russia.

All the Children imitate a cold, howling wind

Imagine if you will, a little village huddled under a pale moon in a valley of crisp, silver snow...

The wind howls to a crescendo, but, prompted by a commanding gesture of the Storyteller it abruptly dies as the children simultaneously blow out their candles

From the dark silence we hear a small group of Carol Singers, singing "The First Nowell"

Papa Panov, an old man with a long white beard, spectacles and straggling hair, enters

The Lights come up

Papa Panov smiled as he worked at his bench, grateful that the singing children had remembered him. But even their sweet voices couldn't take away all his sadness.

As the singing ends, a child knocks on the imaginary door

It had been a hard and painful year.
Girl *(calling)* Papa Panov! Papa Panov!

Papa Panov stuggles to his feet and goes to the door

Storyteller Since his dear wife died, his only comfort had been making beautiful shoes, but he knew soon his old and tired eyes would no longer be able to thread a needle.

Papa Panov mimes opening the door

Children *(chorusing)* Merry Christmas, Papa Panov!
Papa Panov Thank you, thank you.
Girl 1 Isn't it exciting?
Boy 1 I've asked Father Christmas for a toy boat!
Girl 1 I want a doll...
Boy 2 I'm getting a rocking horse...

Boy 3 I've asked for a toy soldier...

Boy 2 I'm getting a rocking horse and a whole box of toy soldiers!

Girl 2 His father's rich. All I want is a golden ribbon...

Boy 3 What's he bringing you, Papa Panov?

We hear the tinkle of sleigh-bells as the Count's sleigh approaches — drawn by four children each wearing a horse's head

Papa Panov Me? Oh... I'm sure he'll think of something.

The sleigh comes to a halt

Count Papa Panov! A word if you please...

Papa Panov Hurry along home, children.

Girl 1 Good-night, Papa Panov!

Boy 1 We'll see you tomorrow!

The Children run off

Count Papa Panov!

Papa Panov *(approaching)* Yes, my Lord?

Count My boots! My new riding boots! I was supposed to have them yesterday!

Papa Panov Forgive me, my Lord. It's my eyes, they're not as——

Count I want my boots! Tomorrow, do you hear?

Papa Panov My Lord, tomorrow is Christmas.

Count *(whipping the horses forward)* Precisely! I need my boots tomorrow!

The Count exits and the sleigh-bells fade into the distance

Storyteller Papa Panov trudged through the thick snow back to the warmth of his little wooden house.

We hear the Children singing "Silent Night". Papa Panov picks up a sewing needle

Again and again he tried to thread the needle but each time his old eyes failed him.

Papa Panov goes to his chair. As the Lights fade the Children softly hum "Silent Night"

Close to despair, he picked up his bible and tried to read, but the words soon floated into a soft, silver mist.

A shaft of soft, silver light appears

Silence.

The Innkeeper—played by the same actor as the Count—enters, followed by Mary and Joseph

Innkeeper Are you people deaf, or something? I've told you! How many more times—we're full! There-is-no-room-at-the-inn! Kindly go away!

Joseph Please, you don't understand——

Innkeeper Can't you see? I'm looking for my riding boots! Now go away, you silly little man!

Mary We've tried everywhere, there's nowhere else.

Joseph My wife's expecting a baby.

Innkeeper She's what? Dear, oh dear, that is unfortunate.

Mary Please — there must be somewhere?

Innkeeper My dear, I'd be only too delighted to oblige, but as I've already tried to explain ——

Joseph Anywhere.

Mary Please.

Joseph Please.

Innkeeper Well, there is a stable round the back. It's hardly suitable, but at least it's dry.

Mary Oh, thank you, thank you.

Innkeeper This way then.

They leave

Papa Panov *(struggling to his feet)* No...no...wait, wait... I have a room. Let them stay here. And I've a blanket, a nice warm—gone... where...where've they gone...?

The Children imitate a strange, cold wind

The three Kings appear

Who... who are you?

King 1 We are the three Kings.

King 2 We have travelled far, bearing priceless gifts for the little Prince.

King 3 I bring Gold.

King 1 I bring Frankincense.

King 2 I bring Myrrh.

King 3 And who are you?

Papa Panov Me? Oh, I'm nobody. Well, I'm certainly no King.

King 1 Surely you have a gift for the Prince of Peace?

Papa Panov I'm only a poor shoemaker. What can I...? No, no, don't go! Take me with you. Take me to Bethlehem. Please...

King 3 Our journey is long, and you are too old.

Papa Panov Old? Too old? Well, yes. Yes, I suppose I am.

King 2 quickly confers with his colleagues

King 2 Perhaps it would be better if He came to see you.

Papa Panov Who? Jesus?

King 1 Tomorrow. He will come tomorrow. On Christmas Day.

King 2 Be sure to be ready.

Papa Panov Jesus? Jesus coming here?

King 1 Tomorrow.

King 3 Farewell, Papa Panov...

Papa Panov But what will He look like? Will He be a baby, or a man, or——

King 1 God be with you.

King 2 And don't forget—be ready...

King 3 Be ready...

King 1 Be ready...

The strange cold wind fades to silence

Papa Panov No, wait! I've just remembered—I do have a gift...shoes!
Beautiful shoes, the best I ever made. Please take them and give them
to...*(He turns)*

The three Kings have vanished

(He sighs heavily and goes back to his chair) Gone...all gone...all...gone.
(His breathing becomes deep and regular, as he falls asleep)

The Lights slowly come up and we hear the distant tinkle of sleigh-bells

The Count's sleigh draws up. He strides across and bangs on the door

Count Papa Panov! Papa Panov!
Papa Panov *(shaking himself awake)* What?
Count Open this damn door!
Papa Panov Oh, my Lord...

He opens the door and the Count struts in

Count Well man—where are they?
Papa Panov I—I...don't know.
Count You don't know!
Papa Panov They—they just disappeared...
Count Disappeared? My boots've disappeared...
Papa Panov No, no, not your boots—the Kings, the three Kings.
Count Three kings?
Papa Panov Yes, they went through that wall.
Count Listen, you gibbering idiot——
Papa Panov What day is it?
Count Christmas Day—and I need my boots!
Papa Panov My Lord, I haven't time for boots.
Count What!
Papa Panov I must be ready. He could come at any moment and I
haven't even got a proper fire.

Count Now listen here——

Papa Panov And this room needs a good clean. *(He begins to urgently tidy the room)*

Count Papa Panov!

Papa Panov You didn't pass Him, I suppose?

Count Pass who?

Papa Panov Well...Jesus, of course.

Count Jesus?

Papa Panov Yes, Jesus is coming.

The Count suddenly roars with laughter

Count Jesus!

Papa Panov That's what they told me.

Count Told you? Who told you?

Papa Panov The three Kings—the ones who disappeared through that wall.

Count Too much vodka, old man.

Papa Panov My Lord, I swear it's true!

Count You're actually expecting Jesus of Nazareth for Christmas dinner?

Papa Panov Dinner? Oh dear, dinner—I hadn't thought about that. All I have is cabbage soup.

Count Cabbage soup! You intend giving Jesus cabbage soup!

Papa Panov It's all I have.

Count Well, if he does turn up, perhaps you'd better send Him up to the castle, we're having goose!

Papa Panov I'll tell Him, my Lord, but——

Count And Christmas pudding with brandy sauce—will He like that, do you think?

Papa Panov I'm sure He would, but——

Count *(opening the door)* I simply can't wait to tell everybody! Merry Christmas, Papa Panov...at least you've given me a good laugh. *(Getting into his sleigh)* And if He doesn't turn up I still expect my boots, do you hear?

The Count goes

Papa Panov remains standing at the door

Storyteller Papa Panov's weak eyes searched up and down the snowy
   street. But there was no-one to be seen. No-one that is, except for an
   old tramp...
Tramp *(approaching)* Spare me a coin, sir.
Papa Panov All I have is a kopek.
Tramp Thank you kindly, sir. *(He coughs violently)*
Papa Panov Are you ill?
Tramp It's my chest, sir. The cold on my chest.
Papa Panov You poor man. Here...take my coat.
Tramp Don't you need it?
Papa Panov Yes, yes, I do, but... I think you need it more.

The Tramp gratefully accepts the coat and goes on his way

Tramp God bless you, sir. And your family...
Papa Panov But I have no...

The Roadsweeper enters

Sweeper *(calling)* Merry Christmas, Papa Panov!
Papa Panov And to you, Roadsweeper! But why do you work on
   Christmas Day?

The Roadsweeper crosses over the street, brushing as he goes

Sweeper Road still needs sweeping. Besides, I need the money. Got a
   wife and six hungry mouths to feed. *(He sneezes)*
Papa Panov Bless you! Dear, oh dear, you're freezing. Come in, come
   in and get warm.
Sweeper *(as they enter)* I won't say no.
Papa Panov Sit yourself down. Put some more wood on the fire and I'll
   pour us a hot drink.
Sweeper Thank you kindly.
Papa Panov You didn't happen to see a stranger in the village?
Sweeper Stranger? Can't say I have.

Sweeper Stranger? Can't say I have.

Papa Panov Here you are.

Sweeper Bless you. *(Pause)* Ah, that's better. Expecting someone then, are you?

Papa Panov Yes, yes, I am.

Sweeper Someone special, eh?

Papa Panov Oh yes, very special—Jesus.

Sweeper Pardon?

Papa Panov Jesus. Jesus is coming.

Sweeper What? You, er...you mean Him in the Bible?

Papa Panov That's right. I know it must seem strange, but He's definitely coming.

Sweeper I see.

Papa Panov And all I have is cabbage soup.

Sweeper Well, I shouldn't worry too much. If it's hot I'm sure He'll enjoy it.

Papa Panov You don't believe me?

Sweeper What I believe don't matter. What's important is what you believe. *(Standing and finishing his drink)* I'd better be getting on. Thank you for that. You're a good man, Papa Panov—I hope your visitor does come. You deserve some happiness.

The Roadsweeper exits

Storyteller As soon as the Roadsweeper left, Papa Panov rushed around the tiny room dusting and polishing.

The Children sing "Ding-dong Merrily on High"

But every few minutes, he'd open the door, his eyes straining up and down the icy street.

Papa Panov stands at his door

A Passerby enters and shouts from across the street

Passerby Merry Christmas, Papa Panov! Hasn't He come yet, then?

No? Aw, shame... mind you, all the way from Nazareth just for a bowl of cabbage soup, can't say I blame Him...

He laughs and walks on

The Children rush on

Girl 1 Papa Panov!
Boy 1 Papa Panov!
Girl 2 Is it true? Is He really coming?
Girl 1 Is He, Papa Panov? Is He?
Boy 2 Is Jesus really coming?
Papa Panov *(chuckling and calming them)* Yes, yes, He's coming.
Children When! When! When!
Papa Panov I'm not really sure. To be honest, I thought He'd be here by now.

There are a few moans of disapppointment

Girl 3 But He is coming, isn't He?
Papa Panov Well, perhaps He's coming for supper instead.
Boy 2 Father says you're mad.
Papa Panov Does he now?
Girl 1 Dmitri! You promised!
Boy 2 That's what he said. The whole village thinks you're mad.
Girl 1 Dmitri!
Boy 2 It's true!
Papa Panov Well... perhaps they're right. Perhaps I am just a foolish old man. Now please, hurry along all of you, it'll be getting dark soon.

The Children scatter back to their places

Storyteller Perhaps he was mad. Certainly, every time he poked his head out on to the street, some new insult would be thrown at him...

Another Passerby enters

Passerby Here, Papa Panov—I hope He's not wearing His sandals! Sandals, eh? Eh?

Papa Panov pulls a face

And the same to you, you silly old fool!

The Passerby walks on

Storyteller But he still looked. By now it was dark, and everyone was enjoying their Christmas dinner. Everyone except Papa Panov, who—for the hundredth time that day—stood shivering at his door...

The Children imitate the wind very softly, as before

Papa Panov What a fool you are... He's not coming... a dream, that's all... just a dream...

The Lights fade and the wind suddenly gets louder

A crouched, huddled figure appears in the shadows

Storyteller At first he didn't see her—her body bent and twisted, staggering against the driving snow. Except for her eyes and nose, she was completely wrapped in rags. And in her arms was a baby, cocooned in a thin shawl...

Papa Panov goes to the woman

Papa Panov You poor woman... Quickly, quickly... into my house.

As he helps her into his house, the wind fades. Papa Panov indicates a chair

Papa Panov Please... make yourself warm.
Storyteller Gratefully, she sat close to the fire, slowly rocking the child

she held tight in her arms.

Papa Panov All I have is cabbage soup.

Woman Thank you...

Papa Panov There's not much, and I suppose really I should save some, but—no, no, you'd better have it.

Woman Thank you...

Papa Panov Have you come far?

Woman Yes...

Papa Panov *(giving her the soup)* Drink it all up. Here, let me hold the child... just while you eat. *(He takes the baby)* There, that's better. That's better, isn't it? You're nice and warm now. Look, he's smiling. Oh, my dear—the poor child has no shoes...

Woman Can't afford shoes...

Papa Panov But the child must have shoes.

Woman I have no money and I have no husband. When I find work I will buy him shoes.

Papa Panov Reach behind you—on my bench—give them to me.

She takes a tiny pair of shoes from the workbench, and admires them before passing them to Papa Panov

Woman They're beautiful...

Papa Panov Yes. Yes, they are. To be honest, I was keeping them for—for someone else. A visitor, a very special visitor. But I don't think He's coming now. I should like the child to have them.

Woman I've told you, I have no money.

Papa Panov No, no—a present. A Christmas present. Look—they fit perfectly. They're the finest I ever made. Or will ever make. It's my eyes, you see, my poor old eyes.

Woman *(standing, and touching Papa Panov's forehead)* Then God help you, old man. Give me the child.

Papa Panov But you must stay! You can't leave—it's so cold and——

Woman *(opening the door to the howling wind)* You are a good man. I thank you for your kindness. God be with you...

The wind slowly fades

Storyteller They vanished into the dark night as mysteriously as they had appeared. Papa Panov's eyes searched the street for the last time, and once again he returned to his chair, heavy with disappointment...

The Children sing "Silent Night"

Papa Panov What a fool. You stupid, foolish old man.
Storyteller He tried to read his bible, but even this was now impossible... and then... then it happened...

"Silent Night" abruptly ends. Pause

Slowly, slowly, as his sad eyes peered deep into the misty page, the little wooden room was bathed with a soft, silver light...

A soft silver light slowly comes up

Three figures appear from the shadows

Tramp Papa Panov...
Woman Papa Panov...
Sweeper Papa Panov...

The three figures stand in the light, each draped in a costume of gold and silver, and wearing a golden half-mask

Papa Panov Who...who...who are you? What do you want?

They each remove their golden mask before speaking

Woman Do you not know me?
Tramp Or me?
Sweeper Or me?

Papa Panov approaches them, shielding his weak eyes from the light

Papa Panov Mister Roadsweeper! And you—you're the man I gave my coat! And... and you—
Woman I was hungry and you fed me...

Tramp I was naked and you clothed me...
Sweeper I was cold and you warmed me...

They raise their arms, as if in blessing

Woman For everyone you welcomed...
Sweeper ...for everyone you comforted...
Tramp ...for everyone of these...
Woman ⎫
Tramp ⎬ *(together)*...you helped me.
Sweeper ⎭
Woman I have kept my promise...
Sweeper ... my promise...
Tramp ... my promise...

The silver light slowly fades as they disappear back into the shadows

Softly the Children sing the final verse of "Silent Night"

Storyteller One by one, Papa Panov's visitors faded into the soft, silver light.

The silver light fades. Overwhelmed, Papa Panov returns to his chair

Full of joy, the old man smiled and his dying eyes burned with wonder...
Papa Panov He did come... He did... He did come...

"Silent Night" ends as Papa Panov falls asleep

The Lights come up the next morning

The Children rush into the street, throwing snowballs, playing catch-chase, pulling sledges, and so on. Several go to Papa Panov's door

Children *(calling)* Papa Panov! Papa Panov! Come and play! Come and play!

The old man wakes up, goes to his door, and the Children gently lead him out into the street where they make a circle around him and dance in celebration—Russian style—singing "We Wish You A Merry Christmas". As it ends they all shout and cheer

Children Merry Christmas, Papa Panov!
Papa Panov Merry Christmas. (*He turns to the audience and smiles*) Merry Christmas to you all!

CURTAIN

FURNITURE AND PROPERTY LIST

On stage: Two chairs
Workbench. *On it:* pair of shoes, needle and thread
Cast iron stove
Bible
Hot drinks
Duster and polish
Cabbage soup

Personal: **Papa Panov**: coin, coat
Children: candles
Roadsweeper: brush
Woman: baby

LIGHTING PLOT

Practical fittings required: nil

To open: Darkness

Cue 1	**Papa Panov** enters *The lights come up*	(Page 2)
Cue 2	**Storyteller:** "...his old eyes failed him." *The lights fade*	(Page 4)
Cue 3	**Storyteller:** "...floated into a soft, silver mist." *A shaft of soft, silver light appears*	(Page 4)
Cue 4	**Papa Panov** falls asleep *The lights slowly come up*	(Page 6)
Cue 5	**Papa Panov:** "...just a dream..." *The lights fade*	(Page 11)
Cue 6	**Storyteller** :"...a soft, silver light" *A soft, silver light slowly comes up*	(Page 13)
Cue 7	As they disappear into the shadows *The silver light slowly fades*	(Page 14)
Cue 8	**Storyteller:** "...faded into the soft,silver light" *The silver light fades*	(Page 14)
Cue 9	**Papa Panov** falls asleep	(Page 14)

EFFECTS PLOT

Cue 1 **Boy 3**: "...bringing you, Papa Panov?"   (Page 3)
Sleigh bells tinkle

Cue 2 **Count**:"I need my boots tomorrow!"   (Page 3)
The sleigh bells fade into the distance

Cue 2 The lights slowly come up   (Page 6)
Sleigh bells tinkle in the distance

Cue 4 **Count**:"I still expect my boots, do you hear?"   (Page 7)
The sleigh bells fade as the sleigh pulls away